For Jack & Laura
from
Tom Gourdie
17·7·75·

Improve Your Handwriting

. . .

Tom Gourdie

M·B·E

Pitman Publishing

First published 1975

Sir Isaac Pitman and Sons Ltd
Pitman House, 39 Parker Street, Kingsway, London WC2B 5PB
PO Box 46038, Banda Street, Nairobi, Kenya

Pitman Publishing Pty Ltd
Pitman House, 158 Bouverie Street, Carlton, Victoria 3053, Australia

Pitman Publishing Corporation
6 East 43rd Street, New York, NY 10017, USA

Sir Isaac Pitman (Canada) Ltd
495 Wellington Street West, Toronto 135, Canada

The Copp Clark Publishing Company
517 Wellington Street West, Toronto 135, Canada

Other calligraphy books by Tom Gourdie include:
'Italic Handwriting' (Studio Vista)
'A Guide to Better Handwriting' (Studio Vista)
'The Puffin Book of Lettering' (Penguin Books)
'The Simple Modern Hand' (for schools) Books 1–3 and Teacher's Book (Wm. Collins, Sons & Co. Ltd.)
'Handwriting for Today' (Sir Isaac Pitman & Sons Ltd.)

ISBN 0 273 00017 9
G3416:13

Reproduced and printed by photolithography
and bound in Great Britain at The Pitman Press, Bath

Contents

Handwriting is a means of communication, therefore it must always be easily read & if possible, be pleasant to look at.

To achieve ease in deciphering, handwriting must consist of symbols which are recognised internationally and be traditional in form. The symbols (the lower-case or cursive alphabet) were hundreds of years in achieving their final form, largely through the pen which was used to produce them and the manner in which it was held and manipulated.

It is quite certain that had it been a stylus or pointed instrument, like a stick, letters would have been quite different from those resulting from the use of the chiselled quill. It is also reasonable to suppose that had our hand been constructed differently, the resulting symbols would have had quite different characteristics from those now in use.

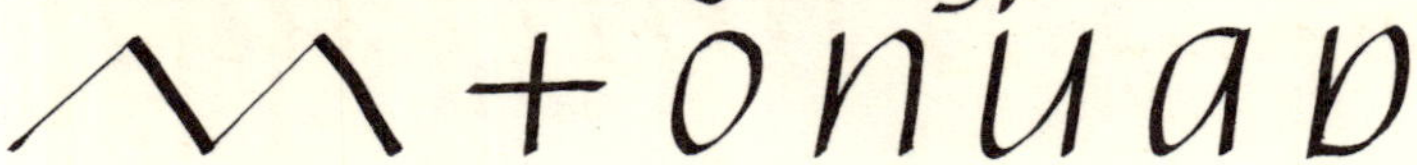

It stands to reason, therefore, that to improve one's handwriting, a study of the basic techniques of the craft is necessary: in other words how to hold and how to manipulate the pen must precede the practice of the alphabet.

When the proper pen-hold has been acquired, then one may proceed to learn how to manipulate it. Handwriting, like golf, requires the same basic treatment, for success in both springs from acquiring those basic skills. As the professional golfer requires to return continually to basic things so it is just as necessary for all who wish to improve their handwriting, to do likewise.

One must learn to scribble as the first step towards acquiring control of the writing tool just as one must learn how to swing the golf club in order to become a proficient golfer. When this ability has been acquired the alphabet will follow easily and naturally and spring from the basic patterns nnn uuu

Acquiring this basic skill (mn, uu) is perhaps not as simple as it looks for it depends on the pen being held lightly & motivated by the whole hand, & not the fingers.

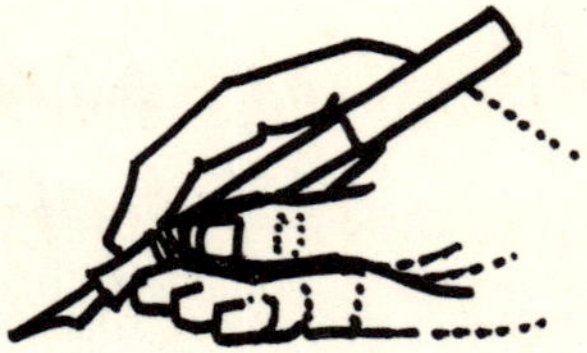

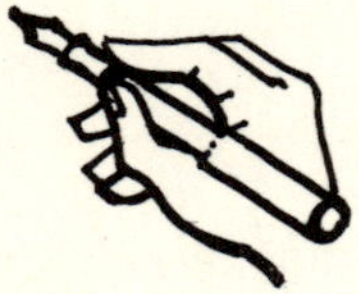

To hold the pen properly it should be held between the thumb & fore finger and be supported by the middle finger. It should point on to the paper at an angle of 45° so that it lies cradled between the thumb and fore finger. This is most important.

The middle finger should be supported by the ring finger which in turn will rest on the little finger so that the side of the hand (crooked like a question mark) lies easily on the paper. The disengaged fingers must not be curled in towards the palm for this creates tension, apparent in the way the fore finger sticks up, awkwardly angled instead of gently arched. If the correct pen hold has been acquired, the hand will appear completely relaxed.

When the penhold has been properly acquired the correct way to manipulate it can be attempted.

If we consider the description of the craft, 'handwriting,' this will help towards achieving the proper movement for the pen must be moved by the whole hand, not the fingers — otherwise it would be more correct to describe it as 'finger writing.'

However, there is no doubt that for the majority of adults seeking to improve their handwriting, it is extremely difficult to alter established habits — but it need not be so if one begins by moving the hand up and down in a nodding fashion, keeping the fingers still. Imagine you are rubbing something out – try this simple movement without moving the hand along the paper, and then let it move in zig-zag fashion:

If your hand is moving the pen properly the down strokes should slope to the right as in my example. By allowing the hand to swing up in an arc of a cirle, the zig-zag becomes the basic scribble pattern:

Natural to those patterns is the forward slope to the right—
it cannot be otherwise for the nodding movement of the hand produces down strokes inclined at about 10° to 15° to the right.

The nodding movement does not mean that the fingers are stiff and unyielding for they must also flex slightly if the movement of the hand is to be easy and natural.

But when the thumb and forefinger alone do the flexing then we get a backhand slope which is undoubtedly the cause of most backhand writing.

1  2  3 

1 Shows the correct slope.

2 Shows the result of not flexing the fingers although moving the hand in a nodding fashion from the wrist.

3 Shows the result of flexing the thumb and fore finger only.

To produce writing of a reasonable size is just as necessary as producing the proper slope for restricted movement results in writing difficult to read.

The basic nodding movements should be practised with a reasonable writing height in view, beginning with patterns overtall, so that one may see what is actually happening, and then gradually reducing them to a practical size of about 1/10" or 2 millimetres in height.

m m m m

u u u u

Handwriting is simply changing from one basic pattern to another, no matter the style — that is, if it is traditionally based — so that to acquire skill in writing one must practise this switching in such exercises as

nun unu nun unu

ama · bmb · cmc · dmd · eme · fmf
gmg · hmh · imi · jmj · kmk · lml ·
mnm · nmn · omo · pmp · qumqu ·
rmr · sms · tmt · umu · vmv ·
wmw · xmx · ymy · zmz

Arrighi, author of the first writing book first recommended this exercise in 1523!

Improving your handwriting also depends on not attempting to join every letter for this restricts control over letter forms and reduces legibility. An increase in speed which produces illegible writing is not of much use but by observing the limit of movement of the hand to an arc of about 3/4" or one and a half centimetres and therefore lifting the hand after every third letter or so, enables one to write reasonably fast without undue deterioration.

Write as many letters joined together as the limit of movement of the hand will allow — and so learn to produce a fine rhythmic flow.

After all, handwriting involves very complicated movements which cannot possibly be negotiated safely at extreme speed, unless an attempt is made to simplify such movements. It stands to reason then that if we have been taught to write a looped cursive hand, we must be prepared to modify the looped letters. By doing so we observe an eighteenth century custom & arrive at a very simple and practical handwriting style.

Change 'aught' to 'aught', 'tough' to 'tough' and 'struggle' to 'struggle'.

It is hardly necessary to state that in order to write freely we must be seated comfortably, with the feet planted firmly on the floor, and with the chair high enough to allow the thighs to be parallel to the floor. The writing surface should preferably slope a little and not be too high, nor too low. A drawing board resting on one's lap and leaning against a table provides an adequately sloped surface which enables one to rest the fore-arm and side of the hand as one writes. The disengaged hand holds the paper steady (placed either above or below the writing) and the paper is tilted up slightly towards the right for the right handed, and rather more so towards the left for the left handed. The back should be supported wherever possible but not be held too upright.

The Styles of Handwriting

The Styles of Handwriting may be divided into
traditional (or practical) and
non-traditional, and basically impractical.

The first fully realised style was the Italic of the XV th - XVI th century which was evolved after almost fifteen hundred years of handwriting practice and in the first writing book to be printed achieved a state of perfection that so far has scarcely been surpassed. The author, Arrighi, had a profound grasp of the principles of handwriting and accordingly produced an eminently practical style which has influenced handwriting today to a quite remarkable degree. Other writing masters produced their own versions of Italic, the best known of those being Tagliente, Palatino and the Flemish cartographer, Mercator.

An alphabet based on XVI th c. Italic

a b c d e f g h i j k l m n o p q r s t u v w x y & z

a b c d e f g h i j k l m n o p p q r s t u v w x y & z , ff, tt

Sixteenth century Italic differs from twentieth century Italic in minor things which may be noted in this comparison.

Some XVI th century forms are still used today but they are perhaps better retained for formal occasions, such as for the writing of wedding invitations, certificates, the transcribing of poetry and such like, where a greater degree of care & formality is called for.

For everyday writing a simple style, involving an alphabet with simple ascenders, should be used. Even the simpler, modern styles all differ to a certain extent and some modern masters submit that a style which customarily uses the special chiselled or Italic pen ceases to be Italic when it is written with a ball point pen. Italic handwriting is not dependent on a special pen —

but may be written with any kind of writing instrument whether chiselled or pointed.

1 * abcdeffghijklmnopqrstuvvwxy&z

2 The alphabet of the Simple Modern Hand[3] is not far removed from the Italic alphabet. Basically it is the same, except for e, f and q and also for the fact that it is written without contrast of stroke, since a fibre-tip has been used* instead of the chiselled Italic pen.[4] This alphabet was devised first of all for school-children in Scotland to enable them to acquire a modern style of writing with Italic characteristics but which could also suit the modern writing instrument – the ball point pen.

Since being introduced, the simple modified Italic has found acceptance internationally, particularly in Scandinavia & East Germany, where it has been officially adopted for use in the Primary schools.

From experience, this would seem to be an ideal way to approach Italic, since it enables one to acquire the basic skills without being troubled unduly by XVI th century mannerisms.

It, of course, must now be regarded as a style in its own right & especially for use with modern writing instruments.

On this page three variations of Italic have been used:

1 & 4: Simple Modern Hand

2 · Formal Italic

3 Modern Italic

The Simple Modern Hand

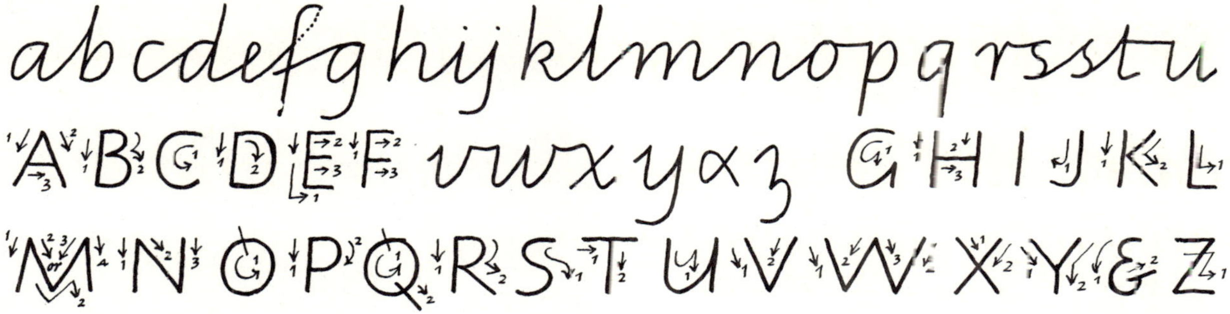

The alphabet is based on the two natural movements of handwriting

m and u

which, therefore, must be fully mastered before beginning to learn the alphabet. All the letters are so devised that they flow smoothly from one to another as far as possible, but some do not join and they are: b g j p q s x y. They, however, serve to provide natural 'breathing' places where the pen is lifted and the hand allowed to relax briefly.

Diagonal joins follow a c d e h i k l m n u and horizontal joins follow f o r t v w to most letters except e which, except when it follows f, should be left unjoined: oe, re, te, ve, we. The only looped letters are e f z. Use the simple forms of f & z when there is no need to loop: for, jazz.

The capitals are only three quarters as tall as the small letter ascenders: A b C d E f G The capitals may be given 'swash' characteristics by writing the simple block capitals much more freely

A B C D E F G H I J J K L L
M N O P Q R S T U V W
X Y Z

Pens: This style of handwriting may be written with any kind of pen (it is especially suited to the ball-point) but it also lends itself to the Italic pen whose contrasting strokes give it an added attraction. This is an example of the style written with the Italic pen.

Practise: ama, bmb, cmc, dmd, eme, fmf, gmg, hmh, etc

Chart for the Simple Modern Hand.

In 1963, at the invitation of the Swedish Board of Education, I lectured on the Simple Modern Hand which was devised for use in Edinburgh Schools in 1962. The style was introduced experimentally to the schools of Sweden under the guidance of Monica Ekstrom and is now, slightly modified,* the official handwriting style for Primary Schools throughout Sweden. Much of the drive towards this ideal step in education has come from Dr. Bror Zachrisson, Director of the Graphic Institute, Stockholm.

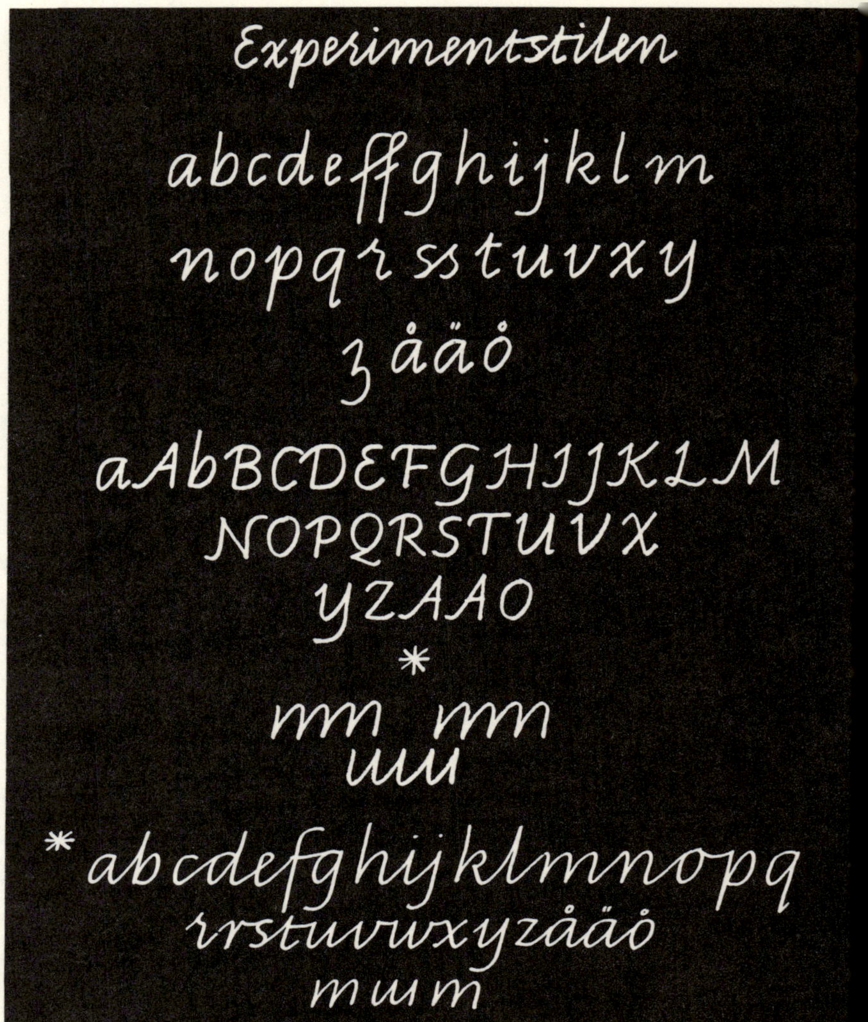

1) abbcdefghhijkkllmnopqrſstuvwxyz

2) abcdefghijklmnopqurrstuvwxyz

3) abcdefghijklmnopqurstuvwxyz

Copperplate & Looped Cursive writing were derived from Italic but were intended to be written with a pointed, flexible nib which, by variation of pressure, would produce thin and thick strokes – a technique at variance with the more practical chiselled nib used for Italic. Apart from that, the XVIII th century Copperplate was a practical style, and sensible, since one was presented with alternative forms particularly to the ascender letters.

1) shows the XVIII th century Copperplate with its extreme slope (almost of 45°).

2) shows the XIX th century Looped Cursive, with a 'cord' line.

3) shows a suggested XX th century alphabet.

The Palmer Handwriting system is an extremely elaborate system much used in the United States but giving way before the simpler styles of today. In it, joins are made whenever possible, even from the capitals and a peculiar 'boat-shaped' ligature is made for this purpose. It would not seem to be an ideal hand for legibility combined with speed, and this no doubt accounts for much of the illegible writing associated with the Americans.

Aa Bb Cc Dd Ee Ff Gg

Hh Kk Ll Mm Nn

Oo Pp Qq Rr Ss Tt Uu

Vv Ww Xx Yy Zz

The Palmer System.

Direct Oval Group	O - O C E A D
Boat Endings	T - B I G S T F
Cane Groups	H - H K M N W
	X - U V Y Z Q
Indirect Oval	P - P B R
Cap-stem Group	- T F L K
Lower Loop	J - J Y Z
Upper Loop	I - I J G L

'Marion Richardson' and Printscript Cursive.

Handwriting during this century has been be-devilled through the introduction of styles not traditionally based, beginning with the Printscript of 1913 devised for schools in London. This eventually led to Printscript Cursive — a contradiction of terms since Printscript and Cursive are at opposite poles! Marion Richardson introduced her writing system in 1935, based on upright & rounded patterns nnn uuu. This has persistently produced extremely immature-looking writing, not far removed from Printscript cursive in effect. She began with the patterns very young children found easiest to make but, unfortunately, she did not foresee the end product. Had she first considered & based her writing patterns on nnn uuu, the results would have been very different and perfectly acceptable.

1 Marion Richardson	One two Buckle my shoe, Three, four Open the door.	
2 Modified Marion Richardson		One two Buckle my shoe Three, four Open the door.

So much that goes under the name of handwriting is just an almost illegible scrawl, meaningful only if the reader is acquainted with the language and can, therefore, mentally fill in whatever is missing. When one already knows the shape of the word, it is quite easy to guess what the word is, despite gross illegibility — but, even so, to impose such handwriting on friends, as in the above, is asking rather too much! Here is the alphabet.

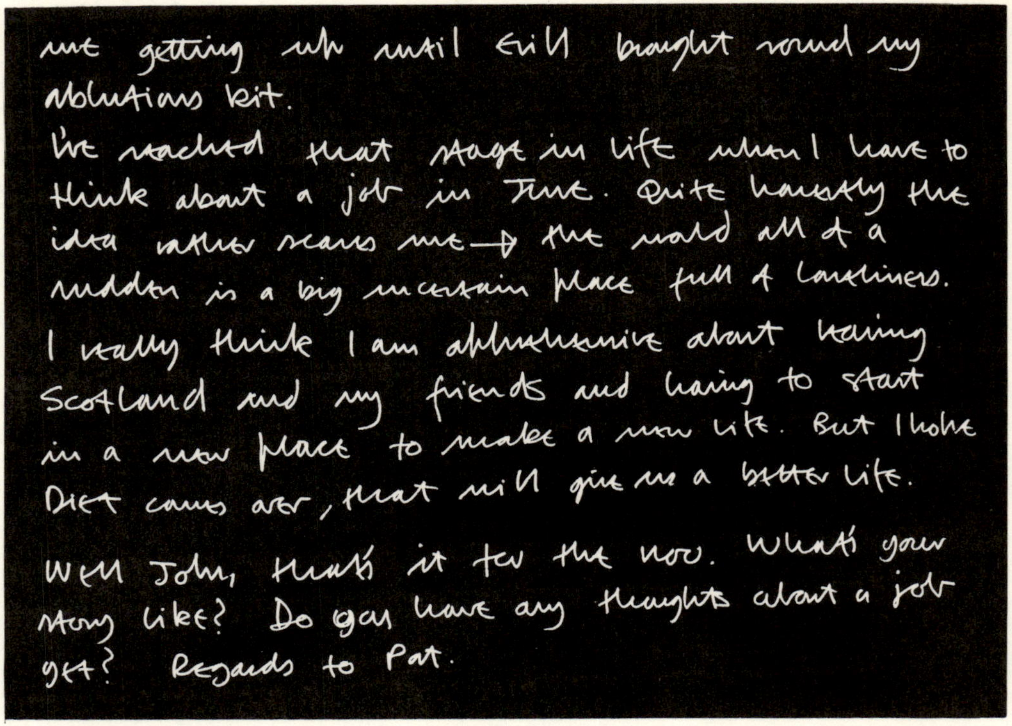
me getting up until Bill brought round my
ablutions kit.
I've reached that stage in life when I have to
think about a job in June. Quite honestly the
idea rather scares me → the world all of a
sudden is a big uncertain place full of loneliness.
I really think I am apprehensive about leaving
Scotland and my friends and having to start
in a new place to make a new life. But I hope
Diet comes over, that will give me a better life.

Well John, that's it for the now. What's your
story like? Do you have any thoughts about a job
yet? Regards to Pat.

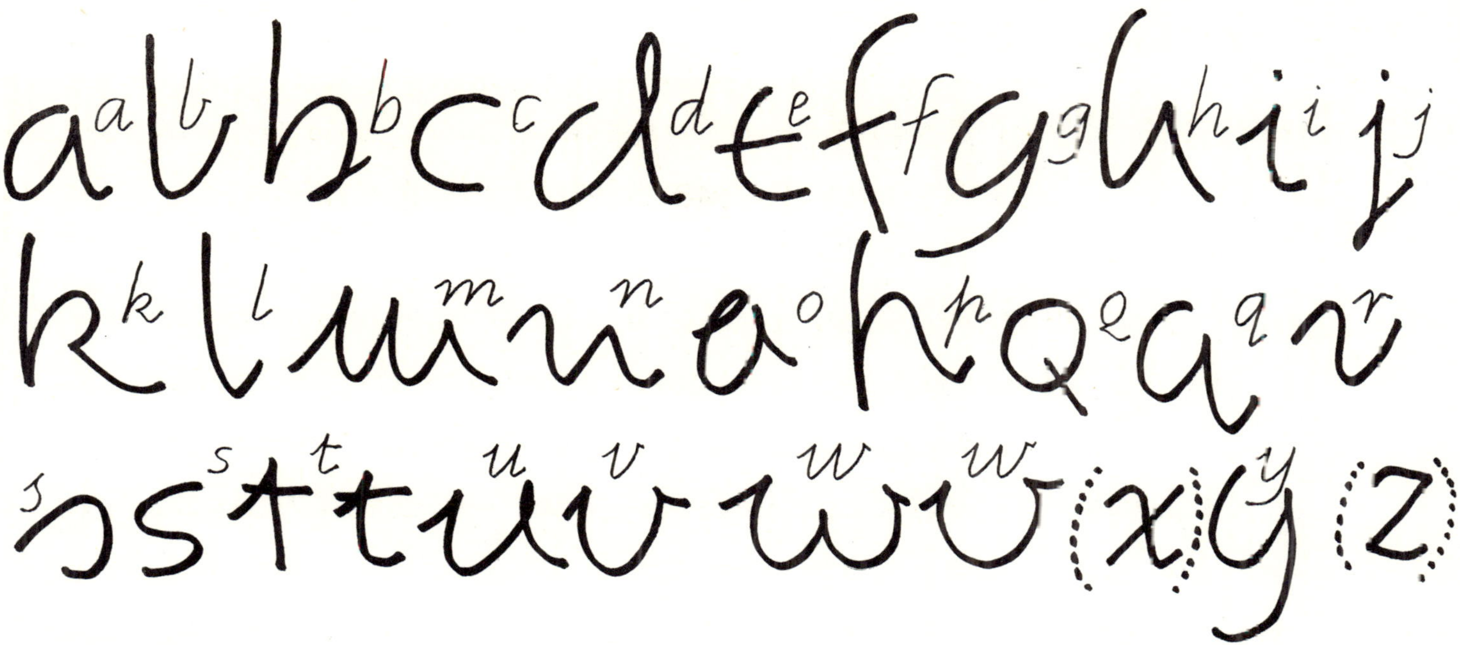

This alphabet might easily be taken for some early cursive – Roman, possibly! But it illustrates very effectively the extent to which hand-writing can deteriorate when it is not based on the proper movement of the hand. It is the result of finger writing as opposed to handwriting. Some letters are so slurred (n, m, w, h and p) that almost total illegibility occurs, making it impossible for anyone unacquainted with English to decipher what has been written e.g. apprehensive, having, thoughts, story.

A comparison of styles, Formal Italic, Simple Italic, Looped Cursive and Simple Modern Hand.

1 Formal Italic

It is rather for us to be here dedicated to the great task remaining before us; that from these honoured dead we take increased devotion to that cause for which they gave the last full measure of devotion; that we here highly resolve that these dead shall not have died in vain; that this nation, under God, shall have a new birth of freedom; and that government of the people, by the people, and for the people, shall not perish from the earth.

2 Simple Italic

It is rather for us to be here dedicated to the great task remaining before us; that from these honoured dead we take increased devotion to that cause for which they gave the last full measure of devotion; that we here highly resolve that these dead shall not have died in vain; that this nation, under God, shall have a new birth of freedom; and that government of the people, by the people, and for the people, shall not perish from the earth.

It is rather for us to be here dedicated to the great task remaining before us: that from these honoured dead we take increased devotion to that cause for which they gave the last full measure of devotion; that we here highly resolve that these dead shall not have died in vain; that this nation, under God, shall have a new birth of freedom; and that government of the people, by the people, and for the people, shall not perish from the earth.

3 Looped Cursive

It is rather for us to be here dedicated to the great task remaining before us; that from these honoured dead we take increased devotion to that cause for which they gave the last full measure of devotion, that we here highly resolve that these dead shall not have died in vain; that this nation, under God, shall have a new birth of freedom; and that government of the people, by the people, and for the people, shall not perish from the earth.

4 Simple Modern Hand

Each of the styles has its own special virtues – the Formal Italic is obviously apt for the special occasion and the rest, because of their simplified nature, are ideal for every-day use. 1 & 2 feature the Italic pen, 3 shows a fibre-tip pen in use & 4, the ball point.

The Alphabet analysed: o n u a ɒ s x — the elements.

The alphabet is totally derived from those elements. By adding ascenders & descenders to n u a ɒ and giving them appropriate entry and exit strokes we obtain all the letters of the alphabet so that it is a very remarkable achievement.

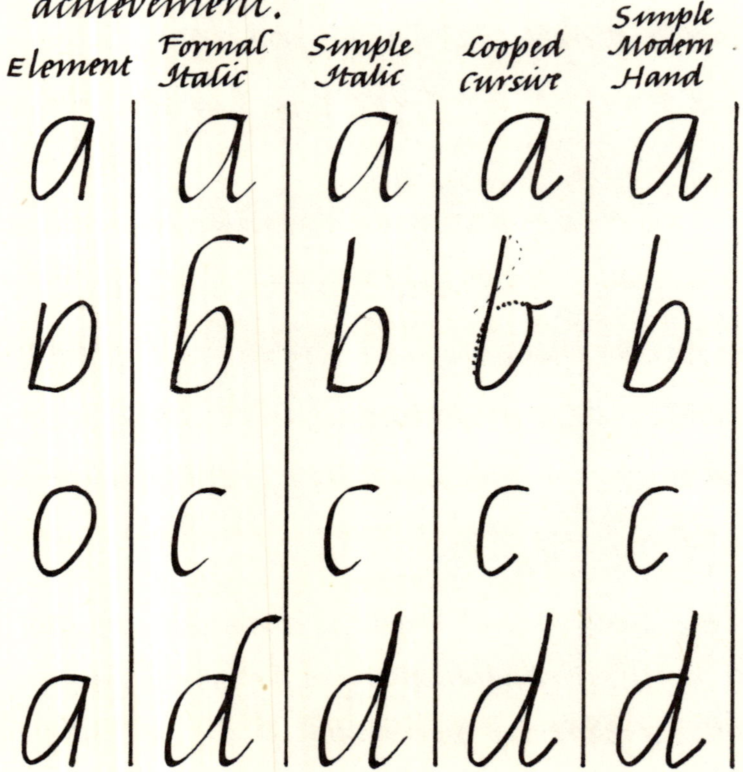

a – this illustrates how a is constructed. Take care to place the letter in a parallelogram.

b – the body of b is simply that of a turned upsides down. The Looped Cursive version is anti-clockwise: b.

c – this letter fits into the oval element but the top is straightened out a shade: c, not c.

d – d is a single-stroke letter except when formally written when it is in two strokes: ɑ l

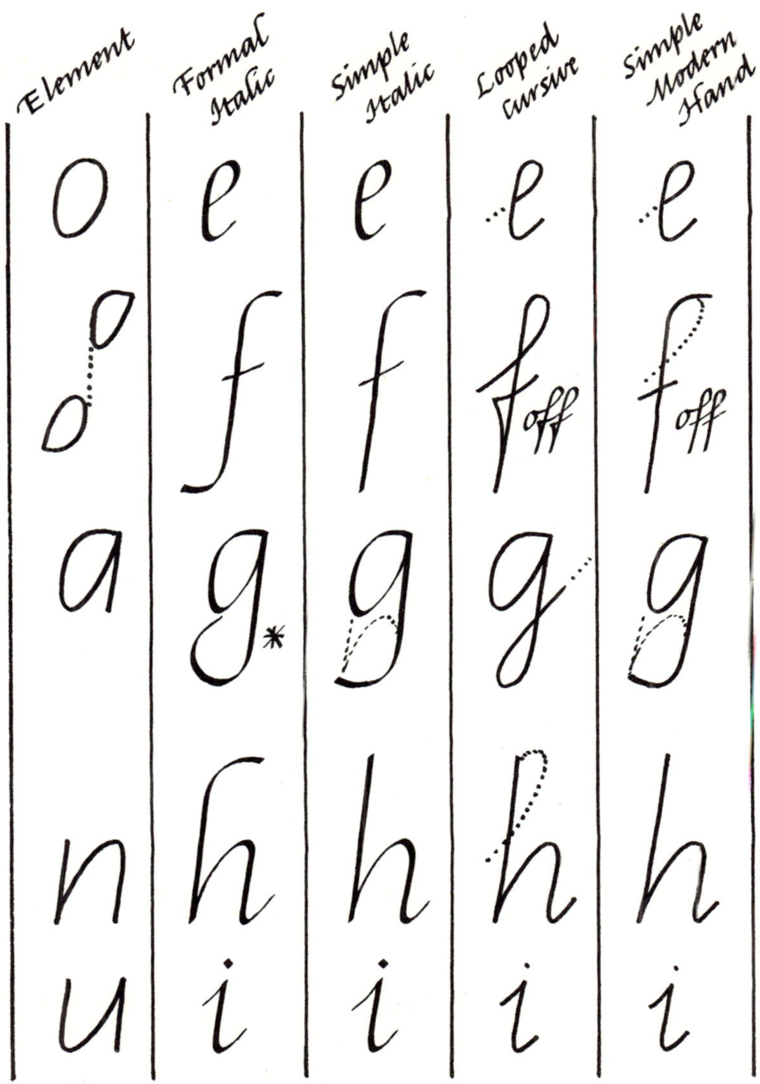

: the Italic version is written in two strokes or one.
The formal e may be flourished: *

note how o and o begin and end f. Double f consists of f and f: ff, in Italic, otherwise it is: ff, ff.

: the tail of the formal version may be given a large loop*. o fits into the tail of g in the simple versions

: h is simply n with an ascender
In Looped cursive it may be looped or simple:
the, when, hand, chin.

i is a simple down stroke. Always dot it!

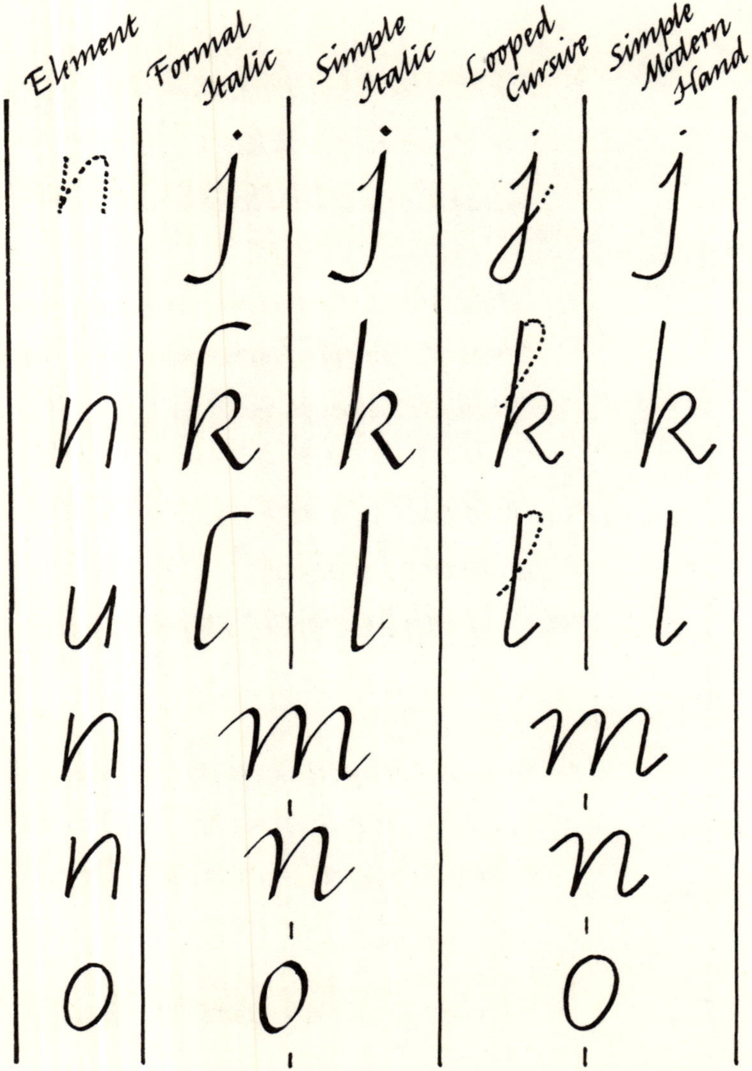

hij When the formal h is inverted it produces i and j : ij

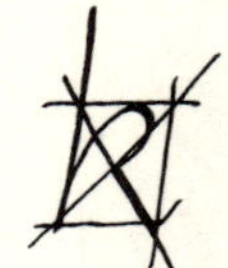

Note how the body fits into a parallelogram with the downstroke coinciding with the diagonal.

l, like i is a simple downstroke.

m is the key pattern of the alphabet. It is the same for all styles.

n is also the same for all styles

O is a proper oval, not elliptical as is sometimes stated.

p must be written in two strokes in the formal Italic. The Looped Cursive p is a single-stroke letter. Two strokes or one is optional in the others

Q in the Italic versions is a two-stroke letter. The tail is attached to O by a sliding stroke

r is a basically simple letter but care must be taken with the arm : r

S is rendered in two forms & is always modified after a diagonal join

t is a semi-ascender letter and the cross-stroke is used as a ligature : to.

U, like M is a basic alphabet pattern.

Element	Formal Italic	Simple Italic	Looped Cursive	Simple Modern Hand
u	v or	v	v	v
u	w or	w	w	w
nu	x	x	x	x
u	y or	y	y	y
nu	z	z	z	z

V : In Italic V may be pointed at the base or rounded. In Looped Cursive it is customary to finish it with an arm V.

W : What applies to V, applies equally to W.

X may be written as two C's back to back in the Looped Cursive version.

Y may be written with a V or U body in Italic. The V version is written in a single movement : y · y.

Z is a difficult letter, requiring more than usual care. One may join from it but not to it : azure. 'z' is an easier form

Letters closely related are a and b (the same movement but facing the other way is also found in pq), ef, hy, un, bq. If X and Z are superimposed on a they will be seen to relate : .

The Capital Alphabet, from 'Block' to 'Swash' and 'Looped Cursive'.

Begin with the simple Block capitals (1), then allow the natural hand movement to take over & so produce simple Italic (2). With more freedom a greater swagger is developed – these are 'Swash' capitals (3). 'Looped Cursive' follow (4).

1	2	3	4		1	2	3	4		1	2	3	4
A	A	A	A		G	G	G	G		M	M	M	M
B	B	B	B		H	H	H	H		N	N	N	N
C	C	C	C		I	I	I	I		O	O	O	O
D	D	D	D		J	J	J	J		P	P	P	P
E	E	E	E		K	K	K	K		Q	Q	Q	Q
F	F	F	F		L	L	L	L		R	R	R	R

1	2	3	4
S	S	S	S
T	T	T	T
U	U	U	U
V	V	V	V
W	W	W	W
X	X	X	X
Y	Y	Y	Y
Z	Z	Z	Z

A B C D E F G H I J K
L M N O P Q R S T U
V W X Y Z

A B C D E F G H I J
K L M N O P Q R S·
T U V W X Y Z

A b C d E f G h I j K l M n

Note the relative height of capitals and 'small letter ascenders, rendered thus for the sake of good proportion.

The Italic pen and how to use it. It is important to hold this pen with its chiselled point so that the thin & thick strokes are correctly disposed. If the pen is held pointing to the writing line & also to the paper at 45° then the strokes will be as follows :

The thinnest strokes ascend at 45° to the writing line and the thickest strokes descend at 45° to the writing line. The horizontal strokes, like the vertical ones, are of medium thickness.

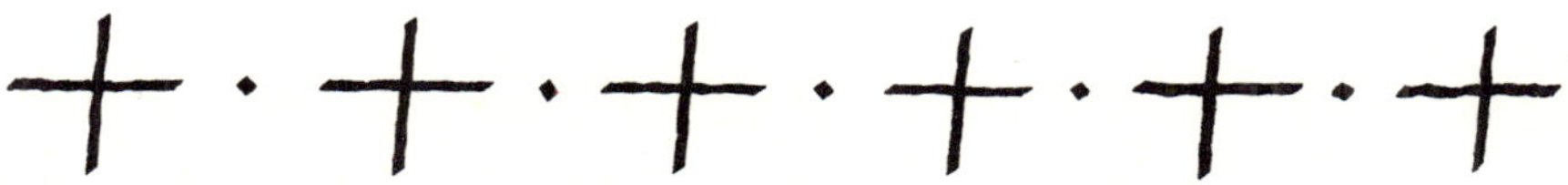

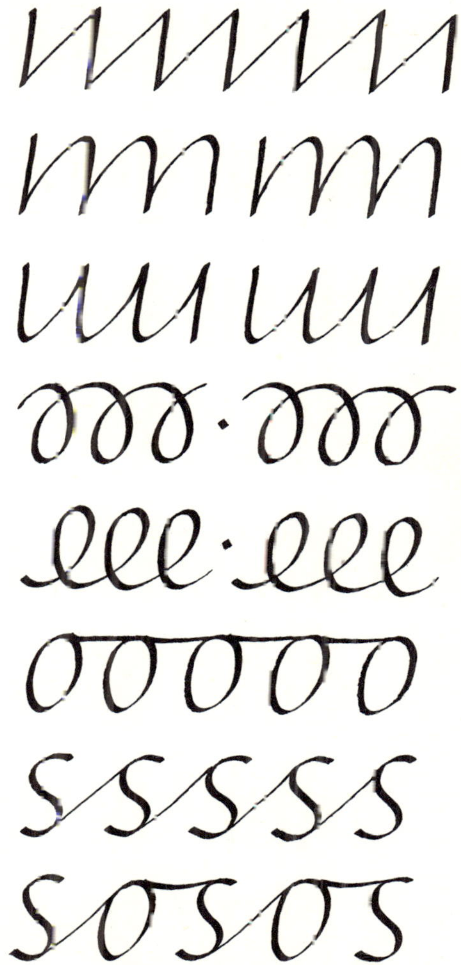

Letter height and the Italic pen

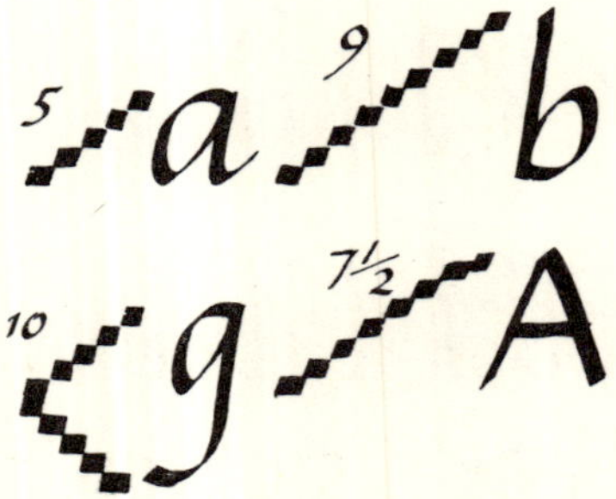

The width of the nib governs the height of the letters in Italic handwriting. The average number of pen widths for the body of the letter is 5, for body and ascender 9, and for body & descender 10. Capitals are approximately 7½. Those proportions may be altered according to the weight of writing required – the heavier the weight the fewer the pen widths to the height and, of course, the lighter weight requires more.

abcdefghijklmnopqrstuvwxy&z

abcdefghijklmnopqrstuvwxy&z A A &A

abcdefghijklmnopqrstuvwxy&z

a b c d e f g h i j k l m n o

Note the upswing to the tall or ascender letters: not

o p q r s s t u v w x y & z

Rules for joining —

Diagonal joins follow a, c, d, e (one stroke version) h, k, l, m, n, u, z. Horizontal joins follow f, ff, o, r, t, tt, v, w. One may join up to all letters except to z but it is advisable to lift the pen at the top of the diagonal before a, c, d, g, q rather than join to those letters: ma, ma. Pen lifts follow b g j p q q s x & y, but when b p & s occur in pairs, join from the second letter of the two: abbey, apple, possesses. The diagonal upstroke is essential for spacing out the letters so it must be as direct as possible. Remember that joining letters is a matter of expediency - Join whenever you can, and observe pen-lifts wherever you must!

Try writing:

abababab a
db db db db d
ch ch ch ch ch
dk dk dk dk
lp lp lp lp lp l
aj aj aj aj aj
my my my
un un un u

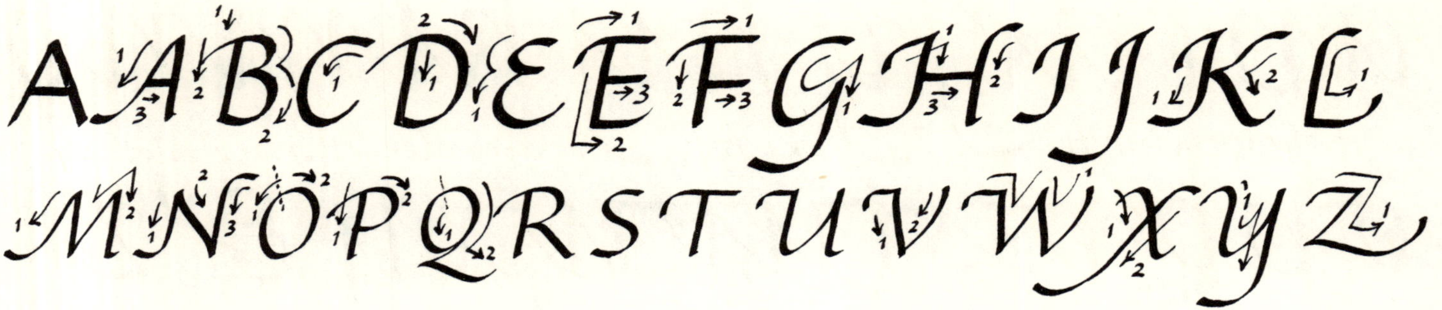

The Swash Capital is simply the Block Capital written rather than drawn, so that it takes on the natural slope of the cursive hand and conforms to the natural oval (O) of the hand when it makes circular movements. If the Swash Capital is drawn rather than freely written then it is no more than an imitation of the real thing.

Used in conjunction with the Simple Italic it gives the simple style added grace and beauty.

The Capitals shown here have been written out with a home made cane pen.

Practice Piece, demonstrating the use of Swash Capitals

When I consider everything that grows
Holds in perfection but a little moment,
That this huge stage presenteth nought but shows
Whereon the Stars in secret influence comment.
When I perceive that men as plants increase,
Cheered and check'd even by the selfsame sky:
Vaunt in their youthful sap, at height decrease,
And wear their brave state out of memory.
Then the conceit of this inconstant stay,
Sets you most rich in youth before my sight
Where wasteful time debateth with decay
To change your day of youth to sullied night,
And all in war with Time for love of you
As he takes from you, I engraft you new.

Are you left-handed?

Being left-handed *has its draw backs for one is more or less compelled to push the pen rather than pull it as the right-handed do & this makes the Italic pen difficult to master. However with patience & with the provision of the left-oblique Italic nib to ease matters, the left-handed have shown that this can be done — and done supremely well.*

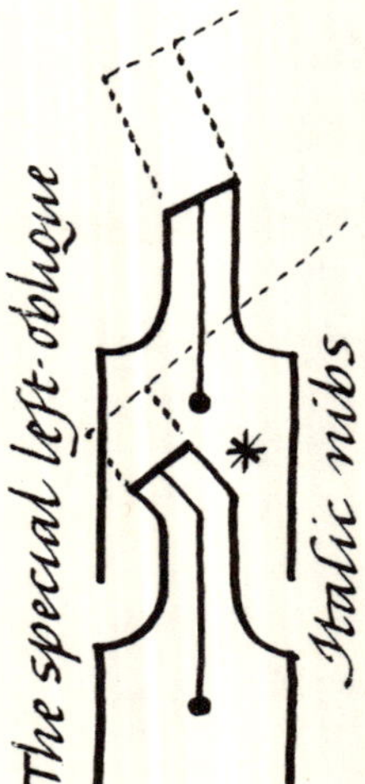

abcdefg hij klmnopqrs
tuvwxyz

In order to experience left-handedness I have written out the alphabet in reverse. When this is done facing a left-handed writer, the pen movement is effectively demonstrated. When using the special Italic pen, it must be held pointed more or less towards the body ↓ in this way.*

Speed with reasonable legibility is not obtained so much from the practice of such phrases as, for example,

The quick brown fox jumps over the lazy dog,

but is rather the result of holding & manipulating the pen correctly. The hand, moving up and down and across the page (with the movement coming from the wrist) creates the basic patterns of handwriting, therefore it stands to reason that practice of the alphabet with each letter interspaced with m (ambmcmdm etc) will encourage fluency and speed. It is not sufficient to produce the semblance of a word but each letter should be clear enough so that the word may be spelt out, even by the foreigner who does not know the language. To measure one's progress, try writing a simple phrase at a reasonable speed, and find out how many letters have been written in one minute. By gradually increasing this number without undue deterioration occurring it is possible to write legibly well in excess of 100 letters per minute.

ama, bmb, cmc, dmd, eme, fmf, gmg, hmh

To summarise !

To improve one's handwriting involves

1 : Acquiring the proper pen hold.

2 : Learning to manipulate the pen so that handwriting, not finger-writing, is produced.

If you write like this you are using thumb and fore-finger to move the pen. The movement is a hand one.

If you write like this, in a diminutive hand you are holding the pen too near the point and pointing it on to the paper almost upright, instead of at an angle of 45°.

If you write like this with hardly any forward movement, you are not relaxed enough and have your elbow too close to your side. Loosen up!

If you write like this, you obviously have no control over the pen, and should take steps to acquire control.

3 : Simplifying the style so that it may be written with adequate opportunities to lift the pen, preferably after every third letter or so.

'Before & after' examples which now follow show what is possible where there has been a very real desire to improve one's hand-writing, beginning in most cases with the resolve to adopt Italic.

At first one can see how the transition is very tentative, with writing that is self-conscious, often too large and without much understanding of the basic techniques. It is a painful process, judging by what one sees! But in due course, when the change is complete, what a transition has been accomplished. In the case of the late Paul Wescott of the United States this is most marked. We see his first attempts as a groping towards mastery of the pen and letter forms with writing that is almost childlike in size – much too large and self conscious. In due course it acquires increasing fluency until it becomes a bravura display of calligraphic virtuosity. Dr Carl Tisch, also of the U.S.A., shows what can be done by a medical man, who, since adopting an Italic hand has been instrumental in persuading others in his calligraphically much maligned profession to mend their handwriting ways.

Dear Mr. Gourdie

What a fine suprise to receive a letter from the author of "Italic Handwriting". May I compliment you here & now on a splendid book wh. this scribe has found very helpful indeed. Yr. chapter on the lower case letters particulary good & I've studied yr. models long & hard. In fact I have the book with me this summer & often ponder it in the evening after the days painting, usually over an oil lamp as there is no "electric" here on this small island.

The late Paul Wescott's hand and five years after changing over

101 Goshen Rd West Chester * January 10, 1963

Dear Tom:

Somebody sent me a beautiful pen & it could only be you; it's so new & fascinating I wrote Jan. instead of March! And I had begun to think you had given me up as a hopeless correspondent But not at all – it's everyone on my list by now who's neglected. This pen will reform me & I hope you wave this sheet in front of the Osmiroid people to show them what a good pen can do in the hands of a rank amateur – in America. I have up to now been using a light little holder with the regular points so this seems big and awkward but in no time I can manage it; how did I put up with the old one so long? thank you ever so much. No more excuses but we have been busy all year – painting, exhibiting, engraving & doing things for other people – all this besides battling one of our worst regular family occasion although Chelsea or Arsenal was more attractive I was glad to join them and experience Division 3 (South). Selhurst Park itself was a great surprise. One expected a poky little ground able to take ten thousand people on gala days, smaller than, say, Fulham or Millwall. It was a vast place. Opposite the large grand stand was a huge, grassy bank with people actually lounging around on the grass enjoying the match from a good position. "Enjoying" was the right word. The football, as such was, by common consent, lousy. Constructive ideas and consummate skills were not exhibited but there was much good, keen endeavour. Defenders blindly thumped the ball up-field regardless of the frequency and speed of its return. Forwards chased the ball, usually in vain. The charming feature was that although the game was bad the cash customers enjoyed it and greeted the silliest incidents with good humour. The ground is good enough for First Division, almost, but first the ducks on the field must be transformed into

Lewis Trethewey changed to an Italic hand & subsequently became an accomplished scribe.

THE ASSOCIATION OF CRICKET UMPIRES

Lewis Trethewey, 42 Lancaster Road, London N18 1HP
01-807 7562.

8 March 1973.

Dear Tom,

Examples are enclosed, as requested. It reminds me that it is twenty two years since I adopted Italic and twenty since my first evening's teaching. Presumably, style has become set and the hand, for all its irregularities and shortcomings, is a stamp of personality. When the example is for reproduction one fears that some vile error or misshapen letter may condemn one in the eyes of successive beholders for ever, therefore it is presented not as my "Sunday-best" but as an honest correspondence hand on unlined paper. In view of these humble intentions, may the scribe be forgiven!

Yours sincerely,
Lewis

Dear Mr. Gourdie.

This is a sample of my handwriting before I became acquainted with the Italic hand as explained by Arrighi and other sixteenth century masters. I fell into this bad habit (I did better when I was 10 years old) because of the demands of my job – a typographic designer and markup man. I still use it to a certain extent that I have never been able to write fast with the broad-nibbed pen. I can feel Arrighi at my back now, looking accusingly and with disdain at this page!

Sincerely, G. H. Petty

Dear Mr. Gourdie:

This a sample of my handwriting after some 25 years of practice. Raymond F. DaBoll, Egdon H. Margo, Paul Standard, Hermann Zapf, you, Alfred Fairbank – there are many whose work I have admired and studied. As you can see I do not follow the rules exactly but have more or less formulated my own. Whether for the best – or for the worse – must be determined by the reader.

Sincerely,

G. H. Petty

Mr Petty hits the nail on the head when suggesting that school is where handwriting habits are formed. But it is possible to undo bad 'teaching' and to begin again, only one must not expect such a formal hand as this to be written at speed!

Mechanics

1. Is all punctuation precise?
2. Are all grammatical constructions
3 Have you varied your sentence st
   some short sentences among the -
4. Is the meaning of every sentence -
5. Have you divided your copy into
   or too many paragraphs?
6. Have you chosen exact words?
   a. Have you eliminated unnecesso
   b. Have you substituted power v
   c. Have you eliminated unnec
7. Have you eliminated wearisome re
8. Have you checked the spelling of

The new 'hand' of Abraham Lincoln is obviously dictated by correct technique rather than imitation of style and will lend itself to be written at speed without undue deterioration.

43 Ankara Ave. Brookville, Ohio · 45309 · U.S.A.

Good Morning Tom,

Your most welcome letter arrived today, Aug. 12th. Thanks for taking time out from your schedule to reply so quickly. I might add that you have one of the most legible rapid hands that I've seen. Your personal style is most interesting. George writes regular but sends his mail by surface which allows about sixty days for some reason. I hope Englands dock workers strike won't further delay his mail. I think George has a very good hand too, and his "blue" ink is almost a trademark. I wonder what accounts for its brightness? He mentions you often. And says he guesses the roads about his area are too hard on your automobile. John Shyers writes quite often and sends me a sample of his work from time to time.

28 · St. Andrew Street · Tiverton · Devon · EX16 6PH

10 · 3 · 73

Dear Tom,

Please excuse me for such a long delay in responding to your request. When it arrived I was away in Cornwall on a course, and since returning have been trying to clear the backlog of work that accumulated while I was absent.

On Wednesday I am talking to a group of teachers at Barnstaple Teachers' Centre about the problems of teaching handwriting. At the moment, in this part of the world, this seems to be a growing concern.

I'm trying to write this at my usual speed, as an honest sample of a fast current hand — warts and all!

All the best for your exhibition.

Yours, John.

Tom,

I hope the enclosed is of some use to you. I'm fast running out of samples of my before' writing, as I've used italic for over 20 years now. The content of the enclosed piece is rather laughable at this distance in time, but it <u>is</u> a fair example of my hand c. 1940.

Carter strode off ~~along the pavement~~ into the shadow cast by the tall sober terrace houses and did not pause until he reached number thirty-five. There he mounted the steps to the green front door and grimacing at the bright brass midshipman who, mounted on an anchor, did duty as a knocker, inserted a key and passed into the cool dimness of the hall.

"Aum!" he cried, encircling a clothes ~~peg~~ hook with his hat.

John Dumpleton

since our arrival here. I don't think I shall easily forget my first acquaintance with the village pub. Last evening, Jake and I, with a strong icy wind behind us, walked, or I should say were swept, down to the country pub, "The George" in the High Street. We found there a comfortable bar warmed by two coal fires, but devoid of any customers. The local brew and a couple of sandwiches did little to restore our low spirits so we stayed only half an hour. It was an exhausting journey back to camp, this time battling against a raging head-wind, so fierce that conversation was impossible.

John Shyvers

To compensate for the lack of training facilities in art schools, the Society, in co-operation with selected educational establishments, recently embarked on a programme of weekend and summer courses in calligraphy. These cannot in any way be regarded as substitutes for full-time art school training and can do little more than wet the appetite of the enthusiastic penman. The rest is up to him. If he can reach his goal aided only by the study of books, regular practice and his own zeal, so much greater the credit due to him.

7 Zwaanswyk Rd.
Stellenbosch.
6.10.62

Dear Ernest,

We arrived back safely but one of our suitcases went astray and it was more than two days before the railway authorities finally came to light with it. Everything was intact. Travelling by train may be relaxing but it's too hot for my liking.

Thanks for helping to make our trip so enjoyable – we look forward to reciprocating your hospitality in the near future. The new house is shaping up well and the builders estimate that they should be finished before the Christmas holidays fall due. Remember that we room for you and even a separate shower for your own use. Will write again shortly.

love from the girls
and yours truly,
Cecil

Cecil Reinfield

17 Coronation Ave. Somerset West, S. Africa
13.3.73

Dear Tom,

What a very pleasant surprise to have a letter from you! It must be more than a couple of years since our last correspondence. I never did receive your letter acknowledging receipt of the prints of the articles I sent to you. Now at least I know you did receive them — contact re-established!

We have moved house twice during the past two years and do not intend to repeat the process — enough is enough. This town is about thirty miles from Cape Town and eleven miles from Stellenbosch where my office is situated. It is possibly one of the fastest growing towns in South Africa, certainly one of the most beautifully situated.

My wife, Stella, is in London at this moment, with my eldest daughter Elana. It is Elanas first trip out of Africa. They will both be in Edinburgh from the 18th March,

Hello Milus

Sounds like you civilians are an unhealthy lot with your measles and all - you need some basic training to toughen you up some. Hope alls well now - ha!

Things here go on and on in a very dull and monotonous way. Wish someone would attack someone - might liven things up some - better still call the whole thing off - I'm about ready to come home anytime now.

Dull letter I know but that's what this week has been DULL!!

Cheerio for now

Buddy

Two greatly contrasting examples of Italic - Cecil Renfield's is racy (like his former hand) while Arthur Davies prefers a more formal approach.

2401 Chelton Rd, Colorado Springs, 80909, U.S.A.

10 · 3 · 73

Dear Tom:

Thank you for your letter. It was good news to learn that you're still fighting the good fight for better handwriting and that another book by Tom Gourdie is in the making.

Your request for a sample of writing before I "changed over," gave me some surprises when I tried to produce a sample. Try as I would, the two-stroke "e," the final "d" and the italic joins etc. kept showing up. It was not accompanied by a feeling of great loss to learn that I'd forgotten how to write "the other way" - ha! The inclosed old 1944 V-Mail, saved by my sister, is all that I could find for a specimen.. will it do?

All goes well here. After the snow and cold of a most severe winter, the brave little blue and white crocus now blooming in the garden give promise that spring is not now too far off. All best wishes from Colorado.

Sincerely.

Arthur L. Davies

eigentlich Deine Aufgabe dort ist. Für das Geld verlangt man in den meisten Fällen schon eine Menge. Und hoffentlich hast Du eine geeignete Unterkunft, und genügend anzuziehen, und einen Koffer usw. es ist jammerschade, daß dies nun alles so provisorisch ist oder auch nicht, es macht schließlich auch viel Spaß oder? Nun vielleicht kommst auch Du auf den klugen Gedanken, mir zu schreiben, sodaß ich über Dein Schicksal noch etwas vor Deiner Rück-

The above defies interpretation without a knowledge of German. The contrast between the old and new hands needs no elaborating

Dear Tom

I thank you for your letter of February 23rd and your request. Unfortunately I find it difficult to give you a letter of mine because – it's merely natural – ›they never come back‹.

Moreover I write very little during the last years and my hand is perhaps no longer a pure Italic one in your opinion. If you think I'm wrong, you of course may voluntarily use this letter.

In regard to my handwriting before I changed over I am sending you two samples in fotocopy. The first one is my hand just before baccalaureate and the other one while studying graphic design. The other two copies are to be dated perhaps 1 and 4 years after changing.

Some time ago you told me you were going to visit Germany. Anyhow your information did not fall into the right drawer as I was moving that year. So I missed to answer you that you would be welcome. Maybe next time!

Since 1972 I have succeeded in building up an interesting job of designing types for headline-fotoset. This is quite convenient to me in many aspects and I hope that sooner or later I shall be able to give up all advertising design.

with heartly greetings   yours sincerely Georg Salden

Kirkcaldy High School
30th. April 1973

Dear Tom,
I think, perhaps, this little piece may be more readily acceptable to yourself as being representative of the College hand of 1956 in Edinburgh. This is written at too moderate a speed to be practical for every day usage. I find it useful at Christmas and birthdays.
I don't really enjoy the effect.

Dear Tom,
I'm afraid this rapid scrawl will bear no resemblance to what should be an "Edinburgh" Italic hand. It will please me however if this sample serves a useful purpose of any kind.

Jim.

O God, what offering shall I give
To Thee the Lord of earth & skies?
My spirit soul & flesh receive
A holy living sacrifice
Small as it is, 'tis all my
store.
More shouldst thou have,
if I had more.

Tom I am catching the 4.30 train (platform 19). – have taken the easel. Mrs. Cook has your money.

Jim.

James Laing,
5, Brunton Place,
Edinburgh. 7.

James W. McFarland, Pittsburgh Pa.

The quick brown fox jumps over the lazy dog.

Pack my box with five dozen liquor jugs.

Whatsoever thy hand findeth to do,
do it with all thy might.

The Palmer Writing of the U.S.A tends to make all Americans appear to write alike and to submerge personality. The Italic hand allows for as much personal variation as one may wish. At first, however, it tends to be stiff & formal (as in Mrs Skillern's hand) but in time it becomes as free as the example by James McFarland.

Six Alma Drive, Pittsburgh, Pa. 15238 U.S.A.

Dear Mr Gourdie,

Herewith is my interpretation of the Italic Hand as you requested in your letter. Also enclosed is a sample of my former style using the common ordinary ball point pen. May it rest in peace.

Today in this city there is a strong movement to preserve the memory of Arrighi, Johnston and others through my efforts and those of a good dozen others not the least of whom is Arnold Bank, a master calligrapher at Carnegie Mellon University here.

I wish for you a successful exhibition and may the result be a renewed and continued interest in this very worthwhile endeavor.

Thank you for your invitation and I would like to hear from you again.

Very truly yours,
James W. McFarland

March 12th, 1973

1730 Fairmount S.-Salem, Oregon
U.S.A.

Dear Mr. Gourdie,

I became a student of formal Italic about ten years ago but did not attempt rapid writing until two years ago. It still is not as rapid as my old scrawl, but the improvement I get in legibility and appearance encourages me to keep trying I only wish I had been exposed to the Italic when I was younger. There is truth to that old adage about teaching old dogs new tricks.

Sincerely,

T. Skillern

March 6, 1973

I am in touch with Pentalic Corp. and hope to have a copy of your book as soon as it is reprinted.

Your new book and exhibit sound exciting. I am flattered by your invitation.

Teddy Skillern

my old school-girl scrawl was always an embarrassment to me. I realized a change was indicated when I found I could no longer read my own grocery lists. Unfortunately I still use this as my legal signature —

Tedro C. Skillern

49, Kensington Avenue,
Banbridge,
Co. Down.
28th June, 1969.

Dear Mr. Gourdie,
I would be pleased to attend one of your handwriting classes at Stranmillis Training College, Belfast, if there are any vacancies.

At present I am teaching in a small primary school where there is no organised approach to handwriting and I would be grateful for advice on your methods.

Perhaps you would let me have details of your books or any other aids which are available.

Thanking you,
Yours faithfully,
James Bell.

49, Kensington Avenue, Banbridge,
Co. Down, N. Ireland. 26·2·73.

Dear Tom,
We were very pleased to hear from you again and to learn that the samples of writing from Ballyward School were of some value.

I have now started teaching in my new school at Poyntzpass and I am hopeful that in the near future the Simple Modern Hand will be established throughout the school. So far some progress has been made and I hope to send you examples of the children's work before the end of the school year.

Margaret and the children send their regards.

Yours sincerely,
Jim Bell.

Some day, when you're feeling important,
Some day, when your ego's in bloom,
Some day, when you have the feeling
You're the most important man in the room –
Take a bucket and fill it with water,
Stick your hand in it up to the wrist,
Pull it out, and the hole that remains
Is the measure of how much you'll be missed.
You may splash all you wish when you enter,
Stir the water around galore,
But you'll find when you finally leave it
It's exactly the same as before.
So, as you follow your daily agenda,
Always do the best that you can,
Be proud of yourself – but remember,
There is no indispensable man.

Both James Bell & Maurice Burkitt obviously derived pleasure before changing over to the Italic hand but, just as obviously, they now find handwriting a much more rewarding occupation.

64, Laburnum St., Hollingwood,
Chesterfield, Derbys.

Dear Mr. Gourdie,

Delighted to have your letter, and honoured that you should feel disposed to request an example of my Italic writing.

Although several years have elapsed since we last communicated, my interest in the art of caligraphy has grown, its use has been a great asset in numerous ways, and I am always pleased to assist in its furtherance to the best of my ability.

However, the limited space at my disposal, which demands the use of a very fine nib, is not conducive to the production of one's best work; consequently, other examples are enclosed, which you are at liberty to use as you desire.

If I can help in any other way, please do not hesitate to contact me ~ I am now retired, and have more time to devote to my hobbies.

Yours sincerely,
Maurice Burkitt

8-3-1973

10

trycheribyggnad. Han presente-
rade mig också för förmännen på
de olika avdelningarna. Då vi
så småningom återvände till M.
Stangler så sade han när han tit-
tat på mitt visitkort. Vi har ock-
så en Valter Falk här i företaget.
Jag måste sett tvivlande ut, ty
han tog fram en matrikel och vi-
sade mig. Där stod Falk, Wal-
ter, A. Så där mötte jag min
första namne – i Boston, Mass.,
U.S.A. Han är av tysk börd sa-
des det och de ringde upp 'o-
nom för att jag skulle få tala
med honom. Han var dock upp-
tagen, och jag var inte just angelägen.
Han var advokat. Sedan samt
liga tre herrar skrivit i min

Valter Falk is one of Sweden's foremost typographers & a lover of fine calligraphy.

Bromma · Sweden 1973-05-15

Dear Tom!

Thank you for your kind letter some weeks ago
and for an earlier one. It is so difficult to get time
to write letters, especially as I am just now finishing
the copy for my book about printing types. The very
writing is finished, but now I have to read it through
and make some corrections and additions before leaving
it to the publishers. Finally it remains to compile a
very comprehensive type specimen part. To show you
how the book is built up I enclose a translation of the
contents.

As always your activities are many –(el) exhibi-
tions and writing of books. The books you have
written now must be numerous.

I am sorry to hear that BZ's article was so

CC: Chest discomfort – few hours duration.

PI: The pt. was well until about 9AM on the
when he began to feel some epigastric disc
he had to "burp" but couldn't. He began
At that time he was with the plant nurse
like the looks of him. She took his blood pre
was satisfactory but suggested that he co
for a cardiogram. He had also eaten an
attempt to "raise the burp" – without succ
brought him to the hospital where he sudd
of pain going down his left arm and coll
Emergency Room. A "code 9" was calle
determined that he was in ventricular fib
he was resuscitated after shock of 200 jou
He has no past history of chest discom
of breath or ankle swelling.

P.H. 1958 – Acute epididymitis – B.H. – O.
1959 – said he had an ulcer diagnosed.
1965 – Foreign body – E.R., B.H.

Form 35

Dr Carl Tisch, U.S.A.

78 Belcher Ave. Brockton, Mass. 02401
9 May 1973

Dear Tom,

It has taken an intensive search to find examples of my old handwriting. I finally had to make a photocopy of an old hospital record which I hope you will find useful.

My class in italic is going well. I have 25 students who are quite enthusiastic. They range from late teens into the sixties, and are from all walks of life. One is an educational consultant from Britain who, seeing schoolchildren there doing it, felt that he ought to be able to. We are using your book as a guide – "Handwriting for Today" with encouraging results. Perhaps I will be able to send you some samples of their work.

I hope this finds you all well.

With best wishes
Carl

Some people, on having been bitten by the Italic bug, have become most ardent protagonists of the style and one such is Fred Eager, who, through his books and teaching has endeavoured to spread the Italic hand throughout the United States. The cause of fine writing owes much to the dedication of Fred Eager.

To stimulate this oneness with life, with growth, education must not seem to the child a necessary evil. Emphasis shouldn't be on books and learning of facts - but on attitudes and aims of life. Learning should be a pleasure - based on the thrill of discovery and of contributing something new.

The age to which this education should go is a debatable point. I feel that ~~compulsory~~ education should be available to the individual until the time he is able to adequately cope with society.

29 Ridgeway ~ Greenwich ~ Connecticut 06830 ~ USA

Dear Mr. Gourdie,

I have been working with Italic Handwriting for almost 20 years, studying, teaching, authoring, publishing, and I'm still making new discoveries about the hand itself and of better ways to teach it.

There is a wonderful friendship between those who have been struck by the Italic hand. They may disagree about some things, but absolute conformity would be dull, enervating, deadly.

Best wishes on your new project!

Sincerely yours,

Fred Eager

Roughly speaking, that was year 1945. On 1st Jan 1946 I worked all day in the Russell Memorial Hall for our dance at night. Everything was delayed and we didnt finish till 5.30. I was to be up at the Manse at 6.30 for dinner. I was there on the dot dressed in Malborough. First I met Mr. Oliphant a very beautifull speaker, then Sheila, Pat, and Mrs Oliphant. Dinner was a success, and so was the dance. It was difficult trying to dance

Art Department. Jordanhill College of Education Glasgow.
7th March, 1973

Dear Tom,

I have never made any claims to be a good calligrapher but I am in no doubt at all that my present writing is more legible and attractive than my scribbles of former years. I was in my late twenties when I made the changeover, and my only regrets are that I had not been taught the simple modern hand by a competent tutor, and that the italic style had not been part of my early training at school. As your expert eye will already have discovered, I am self-taught, and I lack a clear fluent style. Speed is, of course, a relative thing, but I do feel the need for my writing to keep pace with my thoughts and I am happier with a ball-point pen when taking notes, making a rough outline for an article, etc. When time is no object I get great pleasure from my italic nib.

I am making enquiries about the two books which have gone astray and will forward them to you if they are still in the College.

Yours sincerely
Russell Thomson

Without the advocacy of lecturers, such as Russell Thomson, many a teacher would not have made contact with the Italic hand. The pity is that far too many Colleges of Education lack lecturers competent enough to train young teachers in handwriting principles and technique.

March 21, 1946

Dear Mr. Allen:

I have been referred by This Week Magazine to you for the information I desire, and am hoping that you will be able to supply same.

I am an amateur ciné fan, and ever since I read your short short "Case Cools Off" over five years ago, it has haunted me with its possibilities as a movie. Being an artist by trade, pictures have conjured in my brain as to the visual aspect and approach, and having returned from over two years in the service, I am hoping that I can make the film.

I understand I must have the necessary permission from you, and so would like to make the necessary arrangements in obtaining the motion picture rights.

The picture, being made as an amateur film would not involve any financial gain to myself, but if it turned out that it could be of some

(next page)

11 April, 1973

Dear Tom: It is unbelievable that a year has passed since our visit. The press of work since we came home has made the days fly and only when our friend's need is so great, do we stir ourselves. A sad commentary, for as I think I wrote, the time spent in Scotland is unforgettable. The fine calendar with its photographs renew every moment and we thank you for it.

As to your request, it has been difficult to find before writing as Margie refuses to part with her love letters. I did find one, enclosed, written in 1946, four years before I became interested in calligraphy and hope it will do. The only reason for its existence, is that the person addressed could not be found and it was returned.

I admire your great energy and dedication to your work, a fitting example, that I'm trying to follow. When Columbia Studios moved to the Warner Bros. facility, I returned to my studio at home, and it has been busy – too busy –

Maury Nemoy (U.S.A)

AMERICAN EMBASSY

OFFICE OF THE NAVAL ATTACHE
LONDON

25 July, 1936

Dear Mother and Father:

The last letter that came from you from
told of your trip to Tia Juana and had t
snapshot of you both with the donkey. It
like a fine trip and I should think yo
enjoying it very much.

Admiral and Mrs Alfred Johnson came
here on their way to see Caroline in .
They said they had seen you before sa
and were so sorry that you hadn't
in this direction instead of going to
Admiral Johnson has been on this board
reform selection. The recommendation now is
lieutenants be automatically made Lt
after 8 years service in grade and that se
come from Lt. Cdr to Comdr as before. It
become a law before February so I shall undoubtedly
go before the board next Feby. I think that everyone

2945 Garfield Terrace, N.W.
Washington, D.C. 20008
10 March, 1973

Tom Gourdie, Esq., M.B.E.
2 Douglas Street
Kirkcaldy, Scotland

Dear Tom:

Thank you for your letter.

The only example of my pre-Italic hand I could locate is enclosed.

Do please let me know when the new book is published. I shall look forward to seeing it.

Could the handwriting exhibition tour the U.S.?

Yours very sincerely,
Elliott Strauss

P.O. Box 1167
Johannesburg
29.9.53

Dear Mr Gourdie

Mr van Hulsteyn has flattered me undeservedly by suggesting that you would welcome a short note from me. He tells me you are arranging an exhibition of cursive italics to be shown in Scotland, Stockholm and Ohio. There is a small though very keen nucleus of writing enthusiasts in this country and I think it will increase quite rapidly, thanks very largely to Mr van Hulsteyn's efforts. We have just suffered a tragic loss in the death in a car smash of Pierre du Plessis – a very talented fellow and an old friend of mine; I believe you have a specimen of his hand.

Until a few weeks ago my son of fourteen years had an abominable scrawl but much to my surprise decided to reform his writing and to my still greater surprise has succeeded remarkably well. He is left-handed and writes with the pen upside down as it were, the nib pointing towards his right shoulder! There is quite an advantage in this method since an orthodox nib can be used.

I should be very pleased to have a line from you when you can spare the time and also, in due course, to hear how the exhibition fares.

With kind regards,

Yours sincerely,

John Upcott

New address: P.O. Box 35037, Northcliff, Johannesburg

31 August 1972

Dear Tom

Since I last wrote to you much has befallen me. I had been inconvenienced for some time by a pain in my left calf which came on after walking only a few hundred yards. As I think I told you, I was due to retire at the end of this year, so I decided to have the trouble seen to while still at work. The surgeon whom I consulted diagnosed circul-ation difficulties and suggested a small operation involving bypassing the left femoral and popliteal arteries, to which I agreed. In the event, the surgeon found my main arteries to be so extensively calcified that he had no option but to re-place them. So, after 6 3/4 hours on the table and two days in intensive care, I emerged with new plumbing from, and including the aorta downwards – iliacs, femorals, &c. This was fine but unfortunately resulted in an imbalance in the flow of blood to my legs – that to my left limb had been so greatly improved that my right was starved of its fair share, and was virtually paralysed and as dead as a piece of mutton. The surgeon said he wouldn't like to risk a second operation

HOTEL ALFFER
MEXICO

Eric –

Recibí su carta del 15. En el sobre que me envió le devuelvo la carta a Martin con sello mexicano y todo.

Gracias por ocuparse del asunto de la conferencia en Londres.

Recibí lo del Ambassador. De lo que no he oído es sobre el aumento de L.A. a N.Y.

La pesca en Acapulco fué regular. Lo que he pescado aquí es mucha falta de sueño.

Manténgame informado, por favor. "Respetuosamente"

jueves PM

Sol

GUILLERMO RODRIGUEZ

Dear Mr. Gourdie,

I could not answer earlier your letter of March 5 due to my absence from Puerto Rico.

My interest in calligraphy dates from the day a mutual friend received a letter from Jan van Krimpen. I was intrigued with his writing. From there it was a question of going from the broad-nib fountain pen, to the steel pen and, eventually, to the quill which I prefer now.

This, incidentally, is written with a turkey quill and at (almost) normal writing speed.

Sincerely,

Guillermo Rodriguez

SJR

19-IV-73

Shorewood Opportunity School

Corded Buttonhole

Make a tracing (on tissue paper) of the pattern where the buttonholes are to go.

① Mark buttonholes on tracing, making a perfect rectangle, and letting the lines extend about 1" beyond each other. These extended lines will act as a guide for placement of the cording. Pin tracing to position on garment (on right side of fabric) where buttonholes are to be made.

② Cut a strip of bias, fold over fine cord and stitch close to cord (make cording so that ½" seam allowance extends from the cord. Cut cording in pieces, one inch longer than the length of the buttonhole.

③ Pin one piece of cording to the upper line of the rectangle, with the cord on the outside of the rectangle, and the seam allowance toward the center. Stitch to position between the vertical lines using the extended lines of the rectangle as a guide for the stitching.

4128 N. Larkin St.
Shorewood, Wis.
March 29, 1973

Dear Mr. Gourdie,

Here is an original thought which I like to pass on to my students:—

> Beautiful penmanship is like fine sterling. The more you use it, the more mellow and beautiful it becomes. But, if you put it away to take out and use only on Christmas and other special occasions, it becomes tarnished and dull, and needs much polishing to become useable again.

Best wishes for success in your new book and Exhibition!

Sincerely,
June Morris

In changing to Italic, June Morris has had to acquire a completely new way to manipulate the pen. Her writing at the present stage is too formal. To be really serviceable it must loosen up & become as free and cursive as Mr Wollman's hand.

On the Bulletin Board are examples of Line drawings and Halftone drawings. You should study these examples for each one reflects a different technique and a style peculiar to each artist. Also notice that non-representational works are not shown here. And for good reason — No automobile dealer wants to use this kind of work to advertise his product largely due to the fact that his sales depends upon recognition. This example sums up the reasons why non-representational artwork, in commercial art, is seldom used.

The style of each artist accounts for a trend which develops and becomes popular in advertising certain products or services.

Italic writing can be as free & as cursive as any other.

6567 Yucca St.
Los Angeles 90028
Calif. U.S.A.
March 10, '73

Mr. Tom Gourdie

My dear Mr. G.

I have always been a speedy writer. Many years ago I took to using a calligraphic pen, & with a slight adjustment of the arm and structural changes in a few letters, proceeded to scribble as before. As herewith.

I teach "good handwriting" to adults in this manner.

Because, after all, it is enough to ask an adult to transfer to a more restrictive writing tool (in face of all the smooth-gliding pen tips now available) without expecting him or her to go into kinesthetic training to delineate shapes, counters, angles etc. according to exemplar.

We cannot expect a world of calligraphers, any more than painters, poets or even paperhangers.

Sincerely
W. B. Wollman

15800 Lindsay, Detroit, Mich. 48227
U.S.A.
1 · 3 · 73

Dear Tom,

Thank you for the beautiful calendar that you sent to us at Christmas. The color photography of Scotland's country-side is breath taking and reminds us so much of our visit with you last summer.

Jan joins me in sending best regards to you and your family.

Sincerely,
Joe Firden

15800 Lindsay, Detroit, Mich. 48227
U.S.A.
1 · 3 · 73

Dear Tom,

Thank you for your letter informing me of the new book that is now being prepared, and the handwriting exhibition that is in the offing. Both activities sound exciting and should attract a lot of attention.

I'm afraid that my italic hand does not get the exercise and practice that it should to become more flowing and spontaneous.

Best wishes for the success of the new book and the coming exhibition.

Sincerely,
Joe Firden

Joe Firden illustrates the colourless character of the Palmer system, especially when it is contrasted with the Italic style.

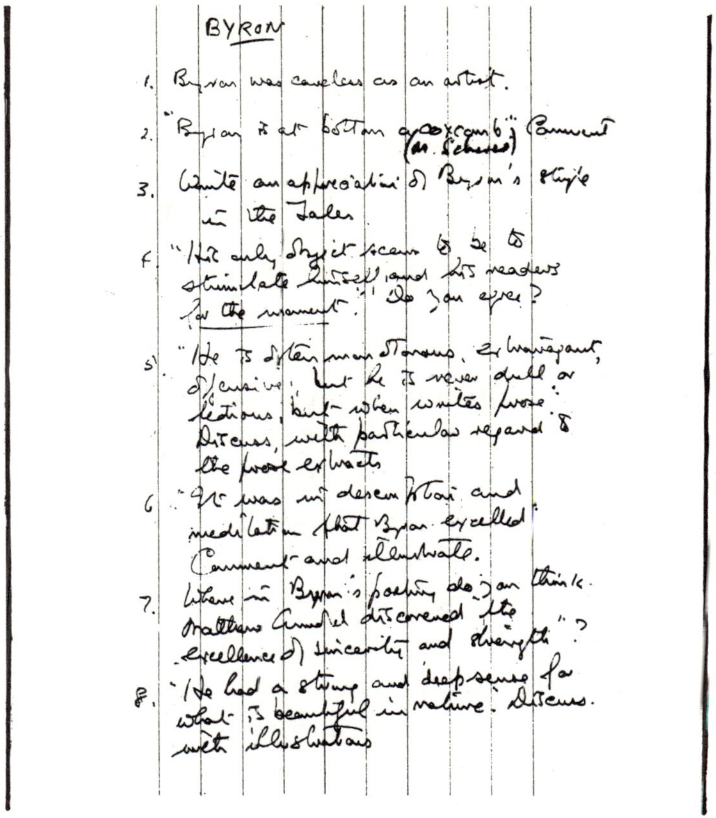

BYRON

1. Byron was careless as an artist.
2. "Byron is at bottom a coxcomb" (W. Scherer) Comment
3. Write an appreciation of Byron's style in the Tales
4. "His only object seems to be to stimulate himself and his readers for the moment." Do you agree?
5. "He is often monstrous, extravagant, offensive, but he is never dull or tedious, but when writes prose." Discuss, with particular regard to the prose extracts
6. "It was in description and meditation that Byron excelled." Comment and illustrate.
7. Where in Byron's poetry do you think Matthew Arnold discovered "its excellence of sincerity and strength"?
8. "He had a strong and deep sense for what is beautiful in nature." Discuss with illustrations

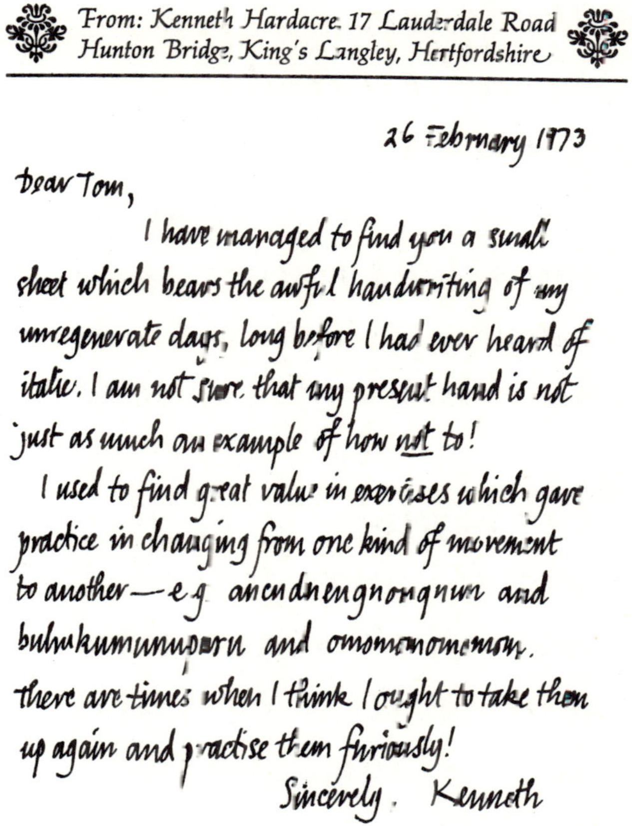

From: Kenneth Hardacre. 17 Lauderdale Road
Hunton Bridge, King's Langley, Hertfordshire

26 February 1973

Dear Tom,

I have managed to find you a small sheet which bears the awful handwriting of my unregenerate days, long before I had ever heard of italic. I am not sure that my present hand is not just as much an example of how not to!

I used to find great value in exercises which gave practice in changing from one kind of movement to another — e.g. ancudnengnongnun and bulukumunnporu and omomomomomom. there are times when I think I ought to take them up again and practise them furiously!

Sincerely. Kenneth

Kenneth Hardacre has acquired a fine Italic hand through following the method outlined in this book.

The Before example* is very typical of the end product of a handwriting system devised by calligraphically unqualified teachers and adopted officially for school use despite warnings that it would cripple children, handwriting-wise. The remedial work to undo this harm has been well worth while and has enabled many hundreds of children to write a simple Italic hand very creditably.

* For 900 years the facts about the Norman Conquest have been in dispute. There are two versions to every war, and the Battle of Hastings was no exception. For the Normans, the Conquest

Sunday in Scotland is the Sabbath, a day you might easily mistake for Doomsday if you were not used to it, a day that barely struggles into wakefulness. Shops, pubs, cinemas, cafés, bandstands, anywhere, in fact, where people with social inclinations might encounter one another, are not only shut but sealed — at least, if not literally, they feel as if they should be. Houses are as silent as safes, and silence is as safe as houses; bottles are not only stoppered but locked; and, in the appropriate season, you can hear a leaf thud to the ground. The weather is the only noticeable happening

Ruth Edmiston
Kirkcaldy High School.

After 3 months from changing over to Italic

Robert Bridges, Poet Laureate, printed in 1926 two Tracts on English Handwriting containing facsimiles of examples that he thought worthy of commendation. In the preface to the first he declared that illogibility in writing to a stranger was an unpardonable breach of good manners. There is no doubt that in too many of our schools this dictum has not been taken to heart. Writing is tolerated that besides being ill-formed, is slovenly, slipshod, and clumsy, and the pupil has no idea that he is forming a habit that will tell against him all his life.

Age 12.

Brenda Kintrea Kirkcaldy High School

Age 15 Senior group

On either side of river lie
Long fields of barley and of rye
That clothe the wold and meet the sky
And thro the fields the road runs by
To many-towered Camelot;
And up and down the people go,
Gazing where the lilies blow,
Round an island there below
The island of Shalott.

Brenda Kintrea has known only the Italic style from the age of 5. This demonstrates the development of a free & unfettered hand.

8423 Swift Ave. Dallas, Texas
7 March, 1972

Dear Mr Gourdie,

I have just read your "Italic Handwriting" and find it both enjoyable and useful. For a number of years I have had a casual interest in Calligraphy, but never felt that I could make a decent attempt at drawing a letter. This last Christmas my wife bought an Osmiroid pen for me, and re-kindled my interest. I chanced upon your book in the Public Library, and decided to try to develop a presentable Italic hand.

As you can see, I have a long way to go; but I did want to thank you for an excellent book of instruction.

Sincerely,
Roy Rice Jr.

8423 Swift Ave, Dallas, Texas 75228
18 Sept. 1972

Dear Mr. Gourdie,

It is inexcusable of me to have delayed so long in acknowledging receipt of the books you so kindly sent me. They arrived August 9th. I delayed 'a few days' to look them over before writing - and the days quickly turned into weeks! Both have been most interesting and instructive. I have your 'Puffin Book of Lettering' and 'Handwriting for Today' is an outstanding extension of it. I particularly enjoyed the examples of your Calligraphy.

'Italic Handwriting', being a later edition than the one at our library, was the more interesting for the added letters. I still consider it <u>the</u> basic book on Italic. Maybe if I followed it more closely, I would improve faster!

Your remark regarding the halting Italic of many people seems appropriate to mine. I can write a fairly presentable set Italic, writing slowly. Whenever I write with anything like my previous speed, though, it deteriorates very rapidly. This is a 'medium speed' version - not a set hand by any means, but not yet a really practical fast hand. I have used the ambmcm chain you suggested (probably not with enough dilligence). Any other comments would be most welcome.

The following examples show writing by a number of people who have decided to improve their handwriting by changing over to the Italic hand. There is no denying the sense of achievement and the pleasure each has derived after jettisoning the old scrawl & adopting the new disciplined hand. This is not a one-sided thing either for just as much pleasure has been enjoyed by the recipients of these letters not only from the writing itself but also from the attention given to the planning of the layout.

THE SOCIETY OF SCRIBES & ILLUMINATORS

11, Dorchester Drive, New Road, Bedfont nr. FELTHAM, Middlesex

13th. February, 1959.

Dear Mr. Gourdie,

In sending you the S. S. & I. Circular may I take the opportunity of offering my own sincere congratulations on your well deserved award in the New Year Honours.

Although you may not recognise any connection with your models, those in your STUDIO BOOK influenced me to change to Italic a few years ago, when I took "ITALIC HANDWRITING" on holiday with me, and covered acres of paper with attempts to emulate your letters!

May you continue your successes. It must be pleasant to know that so many people have re-formed their handwriting as a result of your efforts.

Yours sincerely,

John M. Cackett

Dear Mr. Gourdie,
wegen der Vorbereitungen zur Internationalen Buchkunst-Ausstellung in Leipzig komme ich erst jetzt dazu, Ihren Brief zu beantworten. Vor etwa 10 Jahren erhielt ich bei einem Besuch in London die entscheidende Anregung im Sinne des Italic Handwriting. Wenige Jahre später beschäftigte sich eine meiner Studentinnen, Frl. Renate Tost, in ihrer Diplomarbeit mit einer entsprechenden Reform an unseren Grundschulen. In diesem Jahr lernen bereits 40 Klassen nach der neuen Methode. Für die Lehrer dieser Versuchsklassen war es besonders sympathisch, daß die Kinder nicht nur schöner und schneller schreiben lernen, sondern auch weniger orthographische Fehler machen. Wir hoffen, daß die neue Schrift in einigen Jahren in allen Grundschulen unserer Republik obligatorisch eingeführt wird.

Nun möchte ich mich noch herzlich bedanken für die übersandten Federn. Ich finde sie ausgezeichnet, und werde mich dafür einsetzen, daß wir bald eine größerer Zahl bestellen können. Inzwischen habe ich einige Kollegen aufgefordert, Ihnen zu schreiben. Frl. Tost wird Ihnen bereits geschrieben haben. Sie ist eine eifrige Verfechterin Ihrer Ideen.

Mit herzlichen Grüßen
Ihr Albert Kapr

Professor Albert Kapr, Rector of the Hochschule fur Grafik und Buchkunst, Leipzig, has been largely responsible for handwriting reform in E. Germany

As a result of Professor Kapr's interest, his students, notably Renate Tost and Hildegard Korger began disseminating the gospel of fine handwriting in the schools of Leipzig and district. This became evident when letters began to be received from such as Joachim Kohler, a schoolboy who had developed a fine rhythmic hand in the Italic style. The peculiar German forms of some of the letters add interest to Joachim's Italic hand.

Bitterfeld, den 6. Juni 1965

Sehr geehrter Herr Gourdie!

Natürlich war ich freudig überrascht, als ich vor einigen Tagen Ihren Brief erhielt, in dem Sie mir freundlicherweise mitteilten, daß Ihr Buch „Italic Handwriting" nun auch in deutscher Sprache erscheinen soll.

Selbstverständlich komme ich, sollte ich überhaupt dazu in der Lage sein, gern Ihrer Bitte nach. Entsprechend wurde sie auch von mir weitergegeben.

Da Ihr Vorhaben den deutschen Leserkreis beträchtlich vergrößern wird, glaube ich, daß sich auch die Zahl der „aktiven Interessenten" erhöht. Als einer von jenen, die durch Ihre Schriftbewegung angesprochen werden sollen, möchte ich Ihrer Initiative den größtmöglichsten Erfolg wünschen. Zwar appelliert Ihre Bewegung wohl mehr an das persönliche Interesse, doch wäre es meiner Meinung nach vorteilhaft, wenn die „Italic Handwriting" auch Zugang zu den Schulen findet, zumal diese Schrift eine breite individuelle Gestaltung ermöglicht.

Thompson, Man.
Canada
4.12.63

Dear Tom,

I still can't figure out how my handwriting qualified for the great honor of appearing in the second edition of your book. At the most my hand could be a fair example of the results that can be achieved by writing slowly and carefully. As soon as I start increasing the speed and loosing self-consciousness, my writing is left with practically nothing to commend itself. However, I am flattered that such an authority as you thinks so highly of my hand.

Now how can I get a copy of the new edition of your book? Is there any place in Canada from where I could order one? If not would you please send me one and bill me for it. I used to have a copy of the first edition, but two years ago I lent it to someone who never returned it, althoug twice I wrote asking for it.

I hope the sale of your book goes well as I am sure it will be a big booster to the cause of Italic Handwriting.

Best wishes from yours sincerely,

F.J. Lapalme, O.M.I.

Mount Marty College · Yankton, South Dakota 57078

Dear Mr. Gourdie,

It is with great joy that I continue to be inspired by your devotion to the written word as you pursue your role of teacher in the art of handwriting.

You will remember how you helped me so many years ago that I can't find examples of the "before" which you have requested. When I once realized the value of Italic as a cursive hand, I resolved never to return to my previous style.

Although I have always taught lettering in my regular art courses, my first class entitled "Calligraphy" was offered in 1961. Since then I have taught more than 400 students in 36 classes. I believe the effort is worthwhile and interest is still growing among the college students.

With sincere good wishes,
Sister Leonarda Longen, O.S.B.

March 4, 1973

97. Bandley Rise, Stevenage, Herts
FEB. 24th. 73

Dear Tom,

Here is a sample of my pen scratches! I've been writing the Italic hand since I was 13-14 yrs. of age, but I've no examples of my previous style. It's such a long time now!

I was originally taught the C. Plate hand & changed when I came under the influence of the skill of calligraphy & the discipline of using a sq. cut nib.

Maybe you can find a place for these few lines in your archives?

Yrs. sincerely.

T. Barnard.

Convent of Mercy Buncrana,
Friday August 16th 1968.

Dear Mr. Gourdie,
Once again you have us in your debt. Many, many thanks for the beautiful Osmiroid pen received to-day. It was a kindly reminder that I have been neglecting my correspondence. As you can see by the address I am on holidays in Donegal ~ the holiday atmosphere is not very conducive to the mental and physical effort needed for such things.

I have had very little practice at my writing so I am still quite slow. However once I get back to 'brass tacks' next week I will have ample opportunity of practicing.

I do hope you had a lovely holiday. The weather was absolutely glorious in Ireland. What a pity you did not see it at it's best!

Sister Mary Carmel.

ANTHONY GARDNER, O.B.E.
MISSEL BROOK, CHIDDINGFOLD, SURREY.
TELE: WORMLEY: 3122.

BOOKBINDER & RESTORER,
ENGRAVER and CALLIGRAPHER,
CONSULTANT ON OLD & RARE BOOKS.

July 8th año 1971.
Feathercombe.

My dear Tom Gourdie . . As I was abt. to start out on my 12 mile run this a.m. to my class, yr Lovely book cheered me.

Although in my 84th year I still put in one 7-hour day a week at the W. Surrey Coll. of Art and Design teaching Bookbinding, and I tried to shame my pupils with your book. . It still passes my understanding why all cultured persons do not write calligraphically, especially beautiful women . . But there it is, they damnwell wont!.

Armchaired in a friend's house.

Again, thank you v. much for the book . . 'and all power to yr. elbow.

Yours, w. Blessings,

Anthony Gardner.

28th January 1963.

Dear Mr Gourdie

It was awfully good of you to visit us last Saturday, and it was most enjoyable to meet you and to listen to your talk on Handwriting which was most stimulating and helpful. I am most grateful to you for giving the boys such an excellent start to the term and for arousing their interest so thoroughly.

I do hope that your journey back to Scotland was a comfortable and smooth one. I am finding your book on Print-making very interesting — many thanks for it! I hope that we shall have a chance of meeting again before very long. Thank you very much for your help.

Yours very sincerely —

Robin Treffgarne

20 Riverdale Pk. North
Belfast : 1.1.1973

Dear Tom : I look forward to hearing your opinion of the Zapf piece I sent you last week. For myself, I think its only fault is that it has no fault. Of course it's likely that for reproduction a steep scaling-down was needed, giving the printed script a delicacy not present in the MS.
With this note I enclose a dyeline negative – a reduction of 2:1 – of a valedictory message I wrote, in vermillion and black, for presentation to a departing colleague. In THIS case I do not invite your opinion : I send the thing purely as a curiosity.
May all go well with you in the New Year . . . Frank

Frank McGrath

Servite Priory, Kingsway East, Dundee
August 26, 1971

Dear Mr. Gourdie,

I am writing to thank you sincerely for the gift of your marvellous book "Handwriting for Today". The examples of writing that it gives are beautiful, and those in your own hand are an inspiration. I have the book by me all the time and often refer to it. I am very grateful to you.

I hope that you and Mrs. Gourdie enjoyed your visit to Ireland, and that it was successful, calligraphically.

In conclusion, I would like to say how much I appreciate all the kindness which you and Mrs. Gourdie have shown me. With best wishes,

I am, Yours sincerely,
Bernard Deegan

For even if I am now retired from Konstfack-skolan, I still continue to regard lettering as the most fascinating matter possible. Maybe the more formal letters are of a special interest to me, they always have formed the most important part of my work, but also the sight of a beautiful and legible hand-writing – for instance as yours – can indeed be something of a revelation

I really hope to meet you soon again here in Sweden. Your visit in Konstfackskolan I remember with great pleasure.

My colleagues Elsie and Sven H. send you their best regards and the same do I

Yours sincerely

Eva Billow

Mr. Tom Gourdie
3 Douglas Street
Kirkcaldy
Scotland

Mrs Eva Billow, Stockholm.

"Calligraphy is intimately tied to archery because both are instinctive by nature. One does not write the same way every day. The same thing happens in the perception & judging of distances with the bow & arrow. I believe that a person who has talent for one has talent for the other. It certainly was no accident, or coincidence that Roger Ascham, the first instructor of italic handwtg. for Queen Elizabeth, also wrote the first manual of Archery in England." - Chaly Hauyon - April 1971.

(An excerpt of an article written by Paul Vandervoort II for 'Signs of the Times')

Chaly Hauyon (Chile)

Finally! You may have been persuaded to improve your handwriting for various reasons; at first, the new 'hand' will be stiff, lacking the former freedom — but persevere! Father Lapalme is already represented in this book with a letter written three years later — and the freedom he has acquired is very evident. This must be your goal!

Do not consider yourself too old to make a fresh start. My oldest 'pupils' have both been 85 years old before deciding to adopt a new 'hand'; this attitude and readiness to try something new have contributed, undoubtedly, to their long life!

Good writing!

Snow Lake, Man.
Canada
July 5, 1960

Dear Mr. Gourdie,

A year ago I took up writing Italics after reading an article on the Chancery Hand published in "Jubilee", an American magazine. Eventually I bought your book & a few others. Yours is the one that I try to follow. I still write fairly slowly, but I enjoy every moment of it.

Last winter I began collecting letters (& envelopes) and I use this collection to try to promote more interest in the revival of Italic writing. I already got half a dozen people trying it.

Quite honored I would be if you sent me a contribution to my collection. Would you please write only on one side of the paper because it is more convenient for exhibition purposes.

Thanking you in advance, I remain

Yours sincerely,

F. Lapalme, O.M.I.

P.S. You may feel free to criticize my writing as much as you would like. I am a Catholic Priest, 45 years old, and I use my right hand for writing. F.L.